# TABLE
# TENNIS

# TABLE TENNIS

Donald Parker & David Hewitt·

WARD LOCK

First published in Great Britain in 1989
by Ward Lock Limited, Villiers House,
41–47 Strand, London, WC2N 5JE,
a Cassell Company.

Reprinted 1990

Series editor Ian Morrison
Designed by Anita Ruddell

Diagrams by Peter Bull Art
Figure drawings by James G. Robins

Text set in Helvetica
by Hourds Typographica, Stafford, England
Printed in England by Clays Ltd, St Ives plc


**British Library Cataloguing in Publication Data**
Parker, Donald, *1956–*
    Table Tennis. – (Play the game).
    1. Table tennis, – Manuals
    I. Title  II. Hewitt, David  III. Series
    796.34′6

    ISBN 0-7063-6775-8

# *Acknowledgments*

The authors and publishers would like to
thank the following for their kind help in
providing photographs for this book:
Frontispiece and page 78, Allsport; pages 9,
16, 50 and 71, Alan Pascoe Associates;
pages 27, 37, and 45, Ian Ball, Cleveland
County Council and Butterfly Table Tennis
(UK) Ltd.

*Frontispiece:* Yoo Nam Kyu (South Korea)

# CONTENTS

# FOREWORD

More than two million people in England play table tennis quite regularly and 75,000 play in Leagues once a week, but even these figures look small compared with the 700,000 who are affiliated to the German Table Tennis Association and the many, many millions who play in China.

Table tennis may be the biggest participation sport of all, few doubt that it is is in the top half dozen. Olympic recognition came late – not until Seoul 1988, and despite a remote location and a small arena, attracted the third biggest gate of all the sports played. The World Championships, played bi-annually, will attract around one hundred nations and spectators of thousands on each of nine playing days.

In 1988 in Paris, England played Sweden in the Final of the Men's Team Event of the European Championship and lost 5-3 before 10,000 spectators. It was a rivetting four-hour contest which had a neutral crowd on the edge of their seats. In the same year the England-China matches played to full houses all over England. Television began to recognize the sport. It had arrived.

Donald Parker, who is England's Team Manager and Director of Coaching, joined the English Table Tennis Association from Loughborough College and rose from the ranks of Northern Area Coach and England Junior Coach to his present post. He has played a great part in making England one of Europe's top table tennis nations and has achieved this with a fraction of the resources available to his main rivals. He has gained a reputation as one the of the clearest and most advanced thinkers on the game.

I first knew Don as England Junior Captain when I was coach to my son Carl and it was to prove a wonderful time for English Junior Table Tennis, and the Juniors who came through in Don's time are now the backbone of the England Teams.

Co-author, David Hewitt is a former County Junior Player and a current ETTA Senior Coach. He is heavily involved in current ETTA coaching activities, particularly in the north-west of England.

The game itself is not a simple matter of keeping the ball on the table, though that helps! It can be enjoyed at that level, but the greatest fun comes later, as the finer points and astonishing intricacies are explored. The game is quite complex and that is one of its charms. There is a bewildering multiplicity of spins, variations of pace, tactics and fitness which all play a part.

This book gives the reader an insight to the wonderful world of table tennis. A brief history of the game is followed by detailed information on all aspects of the game. For the beginner the straight-forward descriptions are easy to understand and the numerous good and clear illustrations reinforce all the descriptive points from serving to doubles' play. The opening sections of the book comprehensively cover the basics and then the finer techniques of shots and tactics are presented for the more adventurous player. By the time you finish reading the book you will be hooked, as I am.

**John Prean**
*Chairman English Table Tennis Association*

# HISTORY &
# DEVELOPMENT OF
# TABLE TENNIS

If you become hooked on table tennis, it won't be long before the words 'ping pong' make you shudder.

'Oh, you're a ping-pong player, are you?' goes the familiar question. No doubt, what lies in the inquisitor's mind are clichéd images of some sort of parlour-game alternative to snooker or darts, or reminiscences of a brief encounter with the game in the youth club or the staff canteen.

'No, I'm a table tennis player,' is your curt reply. The images that reside in your own mind are quite different. This is a sport in every sense of the word, involving speed, power and agility not to mention the skill, co-ordination and dexterity that you know are essential for success.

Table tennis has come a long way from its genteel origins in the late nineteenth century as a descendant of lawn tennis. To begin with, it seems to have been largely a home-made pastime favoured by university students. The first patent for the game was registered in 1891 by Charles Barter of Gloucestershire, and about the same time a gentleman called James Gibb – who was a founder member of the Amateur Athletics Association – brought some toy celluloid balls back from a trip to America which he quickly introduced as an alternative to the cork or rubber balls then being used. This move met with immediate success and several manufacturers started to market equipment under an assortment of names such as 'Gossima', 'Whiff Waff' and 'Flim Flam', even 'Table Tennis'.

When hollow, vellum-covered rackets were introduced, the dreaded moniker 'ping pong' was born, derived from the 'ping' sound which occurred when bat met ball, and the 'pong' that resulted as it bounced on the table. And it was Mr Gibb again who suggested to manufacturers John Jaques Ltd that this would be a catching title for their sets of bat, ball and net.

The craze caught on, and as early as 1901 tournaments were being organized with entries of 300 and over and prize-money of up to £25. The Ping Pong Association was formed, thankfully to be renamed The Table Tennis Association some time later in 1922.

In 1902 a visiting Japanese professor took the game back to the land of the rising sun where he introduced it to university students. Shortly after, a British salesman – Edward Shires – introduced it to the people of Vienna and Budapest and the seeds were sown for a sport which now enjoys popular appeal in virtually every country in the world.

Back in Britain, table tennis had also begun to spread outside the distinctly middle-class confines of London and leagues sprang up in provincial towns as far apart as Plymouth and Sunderland. In 1922, an All England Club was formed which boasted such luminaries as Jack Hobbs the cricketer, and other famous names of the time from the world of sport. The *Daily Mirror* sponsored a nationwide tournament which attracted 40,000 competitors. Table tennis was firmly on the map and on 24 April 1927 the English Table Tennis Association came into being, under the chairmanship and direction of the late Ivor Montague, son of Lord Swaythling. Montague was not only to become the architect of modern-day table tennis, but he also achieved critical acclaim as both a film producer and director. At the time, the ETTA had a membership of nineteen leagues; it now has over 300, with around 75,000 registered players.

The first World Championships were held in 1927 and were won by a Hungarian, Dr Jacobi. Apart from the famous Fred Perry redressing the balance for England in 1929, this was to be the start of an unprecedented run of success for the Hungarians who dominated the game throughout the Thirties. Their team was led by the legendary Victor Barna, whose skill and inspiration did so much to elevate the game into becoming a sport to be taken seriously.

The 1950s saw the game turned upside down by the arrival of the 'sponge' or 'sandwich rubber', the revolutionary new material for bats which hitherto had been relatively simple affairs with a universal thin covering of pimpled rubber. Until this time, spin had played only a minor part in a game that had been dominated by the defensive style of play. But these new weapons, introduced by the Japanese, had the capacity to move the ball around in an almost magical way. The ITTF, the game's ruling body, was quick to legislate in a bid to control this new development, seen in some quarters as equipping players with an unfair advantage.

The thickness of the sponge and rubber 'sandwich' was controlled and remains so to this day. But the nature of the game had been changed, establishing the fast attacking speed-and-spin style of our current champions.

Today, the sport both in England and abroad stands strong and is growing year by year. The culmination of this has been its recognition as an Olympic sport, being featured for the first time in the 1988 Games in Seoul. Television coverage of the men's singles final attracted an amazing worldwide audience of two billion! In China, the game is played by literally millions; in school, at work, in the park, at the roadside. Their leading players are regarded as national heroes with 'pop star' status.

Although in England we still have some way to go before table tennis overtakes games such as soccer as 'the national pastime', the picture is nevertheless an encouraging one. With players of proven world-class ability such as Desmond Douglas, Alan Cooke and Carl Prean, we have everything to look forward to. Backed by professional organization, a thriving National Coaching Scheme, an expanding Schools' Association and a lucrative long-term sponsorship with the Leeds Permanent Building Society, the transition from minor to major sport is long overdue. Increasing TV and media coverage means that more people are taking up this fascinating game every day.

Are you one of them? We hope so. You may not make World Champion but who cares? We can guarantee that you'll be in for hours of fun, during which you'll discover skills you never realized you had. Get stuck in and enjoy it!

Carl Prean (England)

# EQUIPMENT & TERMINOLOGY

**B**efore starting to learn how to play table tennis, it is a good idea to familiarize yourself with the equipment needed and the terminology you will come across as you become more involved in the game.

There is a danger, when taking up a sport for the first time, of rushing out and spending a small fortune to kit yourself out, only to find out later that it was not the game for you after all. The end result is that a pile of expensive gear is consigned to the bottom of the wardrobe.

As far as table tennis is concerned, start off modestly. This is an accessible sport and by no means will you find it proves to be financially prohibitive. Look at the hundreds of thousands of Chinese youngsters who enjoy playing the game. The only piece of equipment they have to their name is the simplest of bats that you wouldn't even dream of using to dig the garden with in this country.

Investing in the best equipment does not automatically mean that you will become a great player. Equally, however, the Chinese approach is the other extreme and it is not suggested that you cut corners to that extent. Choose carefully, don't skimp but invest wisely in equipment which suits *you* and which will bring the best out of your game.

## Choosing a bat

Buying a table-tennis bat these days can be a very confusing business, with manufacturers making all sorts of claims about their products. For the beginner – and even the intermediate or 'club' player – here are a few simple guidelines to follow.

***Handle*** These vary in shape and design but comfort is your number-one concern. If it looks flashy but feels terrible, then forget it, this is not the bat for you. The bat should feel natural and sit snugly in your hand without impeding your technique, allowing you to retain maximum control over all your shots.

***Blade*** You do not have to buy a bat 'complete' these days. Most players have them made to their own specification by selecting, firstly, the type of wood and the number of plies to the blade and then choosing the appropriate rubbers to cover it. Until you become accomplished, your major requirement will be control and this needs to be reflected in the type of blade. Go for what is termed an 'all-round' blade of no more than five plies and made out of softwood. If, at a later stage, you develop a fast attacking style, this would be an appropriate time to consider upgrading the blade to one of harder consistency.

*The anatomy of a typical bat.*

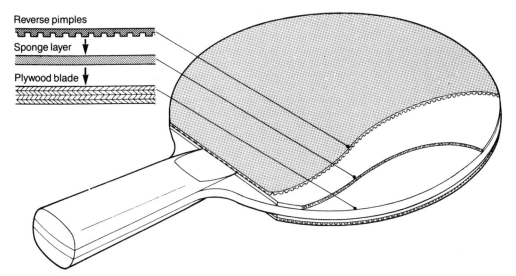

Reverse pimples
Sponge layer
Plywood blade

**Rubber** This comes in two formats – 'reverse' which is smooth with inverted pimples adjoining a layer of sponge, and 'pimples out' which can be with or without a layer of sponge. Whatever rubbers you finally opt for, make sure they are embossed with the ITTF's stamp of approval otherwise you will be in breach of the Laws.

Unfortunately, this is not the only point to bear in mind when deciding upon a suitable choice of rubber. The most popular format is reverse and this can vary enormously in its speed and spin characteristics. Generally speaking, you will find that the harder and thicker the sponge layer, the faster the ball will rebound from the bat. The Laws state that the combined thickness of sponge and rubber should not exceed 4mm (.15in). As a beginner, you would be well advised to sponge layer which is no more than 1.5mm (.05in) thick.

It is important that the overall combination you choose allows you to feel the ball on the bat. Resist being too ambitious at this stage; it's no good buying a super-expensive weapon if you cannot use it properly. In the long run, this will only prove to be a counter-productive short cut, because you will have become too reliant on the bat's properties and not enough on your own technique. The Japanese now have a National Under-11 squad made up of the country's most promising youngsters. None of them are allowed to play with anything but the thinnest of pimpled rubber. This is a material which gives maximum feel and control but has almost no spin or speed quality to it. Their aim is to groove in a flawless technique by forcing the youngsters to play the strokes and not become reliant upon the bat to do it for them. This should allow maximum benefit to be gained at a later stage when they pick up a bat with more sophisticated capabilities.

It is interesting to note that quite a few top players use a pimples out sponge rubber. Basically they fall into two categories, short pimples and long pimples. Generally the short pimples are used by attackers for hitting through their opponents' spin as they have a high degree of control but are not as good as reverse rubber for generating spin. The 1983 and 1985 World Champion Jiang Jialiang was a fine exponent of this technique.

*The dimensions of a full-size table.*

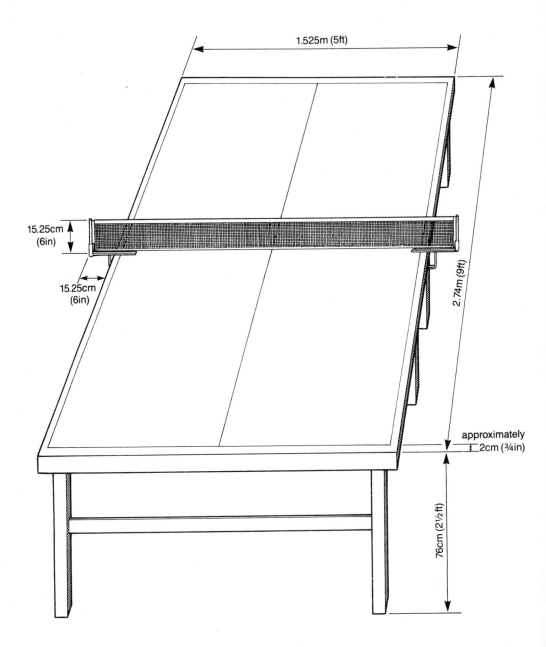

1.525m (5ft)

15.25cm (6in)

15.25cm (6in)

2.74m (9ft)

approximately 2cm (¾in)

76cm (2½ft)

Long pimples are mainly used by what is now a comparatively rare species, the defender. They can be used to great effect against topspin by reversing the spin and returning the ball with very heavy backspin. Unfortunately, they do not have the same control as short pimples and players must weigh up the advantages and disadvantages of all the possible combinations before deciding what will suit their style of play.

## Balls

Table-tennis balls are graded in quality ranging from practice or 'one star' through to 'three star'. With a three-star ball you can be assured of a good consistent bounce with a longer life.

A cracked ball will emit a chemical smell not unlike menthol. When this happens, get rid of it and replace it with a new one.

## Tables

A full-size table measures 274cm by 152cm and stands 76cm high (or in pre-metric terms, 9ft by 5ft by 2ft 6in). You can buy threequarter size versions but you would be better starting the game on a full-size table. The playing surface should be around 2cm ($\frac{3}{4}$in) thick and preferably no less. A thin table will give a poor bounce and affect your technique in the long run.

Take care when storing the table after use. If it's a foldaway with its own undercarriage this should present little difficulty. If it's the loose-leaf variety, made up of two separate halves, make sure you store the two halves with their playing surfaces facing together. Try not to drag them along on their outside edges; this will only lead to chipping.

## Clothing

Looking the part and feeling right can be a real confidence-booster. A pair of jeans and your old training shoes might be OK for the occasional knockabout, but if you're serious about this game then decent-quality shorts, shirt and shoes are a must.

**Shoes**  It is possible to buy shoes designed specifically for table tennis but they are not essential. As well as making sure that the shoes give good grip, pay attention to weight as well – they should be as light and flexible as possible. Support is also important, particularly around the heel and instep. You will probably find that tennis and squash shoes, while giving good adhesion to the floor surface, might be a little on the heavy side. If possible, try to find something a bit more lightweight.

**Shirt/shorts**  Sports clothing is largely a matter of personal taste. Remember, though, that your outfit needs to be coloured in keeping with the rules which forbid white clothing.

Clothing which restricts freedom of movement is to be avoided even though it may look impressive and fashionable.

**Tracksuit**  A tracksuit is an excellent investment which will prove to be an indispensable asset. It is an ideal garment to wear when warming up and easy to slip on when the game is over, preventing muscles from becoming cold and stiff.

**Holdall**  Your holdall should contain all those extra items which you are likely to need in an emergency, the most obvious example being a spare ball. Other essentials are:
1   a towel.
2   a couple of balls (preferably 3 star).
3   a spare shirt.
4   a drink (no alcohol, please).
5   some elastoplast.
6   a pen and notepad.

*Table tennis clothing.*

# TABLE TENNIS · TERMINOLOGY

**Anti loop**  A type of rubber which was very popular amongst 'combination bat' players several years ago. It is very effective against spin as it gives virtually no adhesion to the ball.

**Attack**  A style of play which is usually associated with players who drive and spin the ball at speed.

**Backspin**  A form of spin which makes the ball rotate in an anti-clockwise direction as it leaves the striking player.

**Block**  A rebound shot which is played as soon as the ball bounces and requires little or no forward momentum on the part of the striker.

**Carbon fibre**  A synthetic material used in a thin film to form one or more of the plies within the bat blade. The Laws of the Game stipulate that at least 85% of the thickness of the blade should be of wood, so the scope for using it is fairly narrow. It has the effect of hardening the blade and overall making the bat a little faster.

**Centre line**  The line running down the middle of the table and used to indicate the service areas during a doubles match.

**Chop**  Another term for 'backspin', derived from the player's chopping action with the bat in order to impart a high degree of backspin.

**Combination**  A bat with different rubbers on either side, each with different characteristics producing different effects on the behaviour of the ball, both in terms of its speed and spin.

**Counterhit**  Sometimes known as 'flat hitting', this is a technique used against attacking shots and involves driving the ball hard without imparting any spin on it.

**Defensive**  A term often used to describe a style of play where the player is simply returning the ball, usually against an attacker but without necessarily forcing the play. 'Choppers' are sometimes incorrectly referred to as defenders. Although the style of play may appear quite passive, their clever and varied use of spin and deception often makes them the aggressor.

**Drive**  A fast stroke which gives the ball speed and a small element of spin.

**Dropshot**  A surprise shot which is played early in the bounce and close to the net when the opponent is some way from the table.

**Flick**  A stroke produced largely from the wrist, often used as a way of returning various types of short service.

**Float**  A shot with little or no spin on the ball; the way in which it is produced is designed to deceive the opponent into thinking the ball carries backspin.

**Half volley**  A ball played very early in its bounce. Sometimes referred to as a 'block'.

**Kill**  Also known as the 'smash', a shot which is designed to win the rally outright by hitting the ball as hard as possible.

**Lob**  A defensive form of retrieval, used when forced away from the table. The ball is returned high into the air with topspin and deep into the opponent's half.

**Loop**  A form of heavy topspin used to describe the way in which the ball dips in its flight.

Skylet Andrew (England)

**Penhold grip**   A form of grip preferred by many Asian players where the neck of the bat is held between thumb and forefinger with the remaining fingers cupped or splayed across the back of the bat. The other side of the bat is used to strike the ball throughout play.

**Push**   A short basic stroke, used to contain and control play, often during the early part of a rally.

**Spin**   Spin occurs when the ball rotates on its axis during flight. It is produced when the bat's rubber surface temporarily grips the ball when contact is made. The direction of the rotation is governed by the direction in which the bat is brushed against the ball.

**Third-ball attack**   This refers to the third ball of the rally immediately following the receipt of serve which often provides the server with an ideal opportunity to open an attack.

**Topspin**   A form of spin which makes the ball rotate in a clockwise direction as it leaves the striking player.

**Twiddle**   A technique favoured by many combination-bat players. It involves turning the bat in the hand during the rally so that both surfaces can, if desired, be used on both the forehand and backhand wings.

# THE GAME – A GUIDE

**T**able tennis can be played as singles or doubles and as either men's, women's or mixed. Unlike other racket sports, such as badminton, tennis and squash, volleying is not allowed and the ball must be left to bounce on your own side of the table before you are allowed to hit it.

Most matches consist of the best of three games although in major international competitions this is often extended to the best of five, particularly in the main individual events. A game is won by the first player or pair to reach 21 points, or if the score is level at 20-all, the first to achieve a two-point differential.

## Starting a game and serving

The toss of a coin confers on a player the right to make a number of choices. This can be to serve or receive first, whereupon the other player has the choice of ends. Alternatively, as the winner of the toss, you may choose an end, whereupon the loser may choose to serve or receive. Lastly, you can require the loser to make the first choice leaving you with whichever choice is not made by the loser. If you win the toss and choose to serve in the first game, you will be the receiver at the start of the second but the server once more at the start of the third (assuming the match goes to a third game).

After every five serves, the service passes over to the opposing player and this process continues until the game is over. However, if the score reaches 20-all, service is exchanged alternately until a winner emerges with two clear points. Unlike badminton and squash, points can be won or lost on the service.

There are a number of rules peculiar to the service which, if not properly observed, can be penalized by a point being awarded to the opposing player. These are as follows:

1 The service must bounce twice, once on the server's side of the net and then on the receiver's side.
2 The free hand, while in contact with the ball immediately prior to serving, must at all times be above the level of the table's surface for as long as the ball remains stationary on the palm of the server's free hand.
3 The ball must be thrown up from a stationary position on the palm of the free hand and not the fingers. It must be struck only on its descent.
4 When the ball is struck in service, it must be from behind the white baseline on the edge of the server's side of the table, or an imaginary extension of it should players choose to serve from a wide position.

**5** The server has to ensure that the serving action is visible throughout to the umpire.

**6** The service must not be farther back than the part of the server's body, other than his arm, head or leg which is farthest from the net. This rule sounds a little confusing but it is designed to prevent the server from turning his body away from the receiver and shielding the serving action from view.

**7** If the ball brushes the net as it passes over to the other side, a 'let' is called and play stops. The server continues until a good serve is achieved.

## Changing ends

Ends are changed at the completion of each game and if the match goes to a deciding game, ends are changed when one player or pair reaches 10.

## The rally

The rally continues until one player makes a fault. There are a number of ways he can do this and the most common are:

**1** missing the ball completely.
**2** failing to hit it over the net.
**3** missing the receiver's side of the table, perhaps by hitting the ball too far.

Other less common faults are dealt with in the 'Rules Clinic' chapter.

## Scoring

This is fairly straightforward. There are two fundamental things for a scorer to remember. Firstly, the server's score is shouted first and secondly you must see that service changes hands after every five serves. An easy way to do this is to remember that this occurs when the two scores added together are divisible by five, e.g. 3-2, 14-11, 17-13 and so on.

## Doubles

There are a number of rules which are unique to doubles but which do not feature in a singles contest. These are set out below:

**1** You must serve from the right-hand side of the table and your service must land in the opposition's right-hand side. It is for this purpose that many tables feature a white line running down the centre.

**2** You and your partner must hit the ball in sequence, alternately, until the rally is over. If you hit the ball out of order, your team will automatically lose the point.

**3** After you have completed five serves, change places with your partner who becomes the receiver for the opposition's next five serves before commencing with his or her own set of five serves.

**4** At the start of the second game, you must ensure that you are not serving to and receiving from the same player as you did in the first game. Similarly, if the match goes to a decider and you change ends at 10 points you must again swap places with your partner.

# RULES CLINIC

### If I establish a lead of 11-0, do I automatically win the game?

No. This is a popular myth which has probably been the cause of many an argument on holidays or during a brief lunchtime knockabout at work or school. The game is only won, or lost, when the score reaches 21, or once two clear points have been won should the game go beyond 20-20.

### If I play three let serves on the trot, do I automatically lose the point?

No, this is another myth. You must press on until you perform a service which passes clearly over the net – even if it takes you ten attempts!

### What happens if a server serves before I'm ready?

Provided you make no attempt to play, you can ask the umpire for a let.

### Can I swap the bat between hands during a rally?

Yes, provided you use only the bat and not your hand to strike the ball.

### What if I return the ball with my bat handle?

This would be quite permissible as long as your hand has not interfered with the ball in any way.

### If the ball is played very short, can I use my free hand to rest on the table while I stretch to return it?

No, this is not allowed and would be penalized by the loss of a point.

### What if my clothes or my leg occasionally touch the table?

Provided you don't move the table, you would not be in breach of any of the laws. However, no part of your body or clothing must touch the net as this certainly would mean the loss of a point.

### Can I towel down during the game?

Towelling down is only allowed after a change of service and in between games.

**If I return the ball from a very wide position, it may look as though it's gone around the net. Is this acceptable?**

Yes, your return will be regarded as having passed over the net for the purposes of the rules. It can pass under or outside the projection of the net assembly, although it must land on the table's surface. If it bounces off the side, this will not count.

**I know I have to throw the ball up on service. Will it be allowed if I only throw it up a couple of inches?**

No, the ball must rise at least 16cm (6in) after leaving the palm of the free hand.

*Three typical service faults – all in one! Hitting the ball over the table, without any throw-up, from a cupped hand.*

**I'm disabled and it is almost impossible for me to comply with every last detail of the service laws. Is there any discretion?**

Strict observance of any particular requirement for a good service may be waived where the umpire is notified before play begins that compliance with that requirement is prevented by physical disability.

**Do we play on if the ball cracks during a rally?**

No, a let must be called and play is suspended while the ball is replaced.

**Do the rubbers on my bat each have to be a different colour?**

Yes, International Laws state that the surface of one side of the bat should be bright red and the other side should be black, whether or not both sides are used for striking the ball.

**Is there any time limit on a game?**

Yes, there is a requirement that a game should be completed within fifteen minutes. If it isn't, an arrangement called the expedite system comes into operation. It is extremely unlikely that you will ever need to use it but if you would like to know more, a full description is contained within the Laws of the Game.

**Are these all the rules?**

Not all, but they are virtually all you will need to get started. A booklet containing the full Laws can be obtained from the English Table Tennis Association (address on page 77).

# TECHNIQUE

The path to becoming a top player follows a route which becomes progressively steeper the further you travel. Rest assured, bad habits and basic flaws will have the same effect as trying to climb the Eiger with holes in your boots! The message we are trying to get across is a simple one: time spent on acquiring strong basic skills is time well spent. As you will find out, virtually all the more advanced shots are derived from four simple strokes which in turn are all based on the same fundamental principles. If you get the foundations right, there's every chance of you building a respectable game which should enable you to fulfil your potential.

## Get a grip!

Back in the Forties and Fifties, there were umpteen different styles of grip being used at international level. Variations still exist today but they are generally much more subtle than in former years. Some things never change though, and essentially there will only ever be two ways of holding a table tennis bat – with a good grip or with a bad grip. A bad grip is one which is uncomfortable, which limits flexibility, inhibits the execution of certain strokes, or needs changing between the forehand and backhand wings. A good grip suffers none of these drawbacks but acts as a natural extension of the playing hand. It may vary in appearance from one player to the next, but this will be because each player has found precisely the position which serves him or her the best.

*The shakehand grip.*

*The shakehand grip.*

*The penhold grip. The remaining fingers can be splayed or cupped on the reverse side of the bat.*

The type of grip preferred by most Western and European players is known as the **shakehand** grip. It is achieved by literally shaking hands with the handle of the bat and is characterized by the forefinger being extended along the base of the blade and the thumb resting on the opposite side. The remaining three fingers surround the handle and the shoulder of the bat should be sitting neatly under that area of skin that lies between thumb and forefinger. Try not to cock your wrist but instead let it drop slightly so the upper edge of the bat lies at roughly the same height as your wrist joint.

One of the great advantages of the shakehand grip is that it allows for instant delicate adjustments to be made to the angle of the bat during play. This fine degree of control is made possible because of the positioning of the thumb and forefinger. As you will soon discover, control over bat and hand is absolutely critical in this game and it will be lost if you make the mistake of gripping the bat too tightly.

It would be wrong not to mention the other most popular grip in the game, not least because it is favoured by half the population of China, the greatest table-tennis nation on earth. This is the **penhold** grip, so called because the handle is gripped by the thumb and forefinger in much the same way as you might hold a pen. The remaining fingers either rest or are spread across the opposite side of the bat, which, unlike the shakehand grip, is not used to strike the ball.

*The right sort of stance will mean you are poised for action!*

Uncomfortable though it might appear, the penhold grip has been used to tremendous effect by many great world champions.

## GOOD · STYLE

Why is it that some players look as though they have all the time in the world yet others are falling over themselves even to get near the ball? Unfortunately, there is no simple answer to this puzzle – it depends on many factors and variables such as natural skill, talent and co-ordination. But there are a few key principles which, if mastered properly, will help you on your way to international acclaim.

# TECHNIQUE

*Learn to hit the ball at the peak of its bounce.*

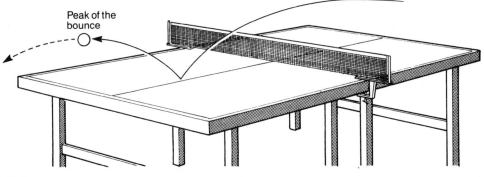

Peak of the bounce

## Stance

The right sort of stance will give you a sound base to operate from. It needs to be one that will help you sustain balance, transfer your bodyweight, keep a steady vision and let you spring quickly and economically to all corners of the table.

Start with your feet about as wide as your shoulders. Keep you knees bent slightly and stick your backside out a little. Crouch forward by arching your back so that your chin is in line vertically with your knees. Make sure that your playing arm is held out in front of you with the elbow bent and its movement unrestricted by your upper body. Your bat should be just about grazing the edge of the table. Your free arm, which is a vital ingredient in keeping an overall balance, should be held parallel to the playing arm.

Lastly, make sure that at all times your weight is on the balls of your feet and not on your heels. If you've managed to copy correctly all the points just described, you'll probably find that this is precisely where your body weight is being supported.

## Timing

As you read on, you will notice that we use the term 'peak of the bounce' on many occasions. Developments in the game over the last ten years or so have shown us that, for many shots, this is undoubtedly the optimum timing point.

It usually occurs at a point which is above net height, and because of this the target area is made bigger, it is easier to make full use of your power and it gives your opponent less time to respond.

If you try to adopt a 'peak of the bounce' timing point from Day One, it should stop with you for the rest of your playing career. This should prove useful when you get involved in a high-pressure game; instead of being forced away from the table and thereby hitting the ball later (and probably in a defensive manner), your intuition and instinct will be telling you to stop up there and fight it out in fine attacking style.

Not everyone is successful in acquiring this habit. Some players discover that they need more time to execute their strokes properly, and therefore they prefer to take the ball a little later. For this reason, players whose natural timing point is after the peak, or late, tend to become defenders and adopt the backspin game. This is no bad thing – you only have to look at the top Korean, Lee Gun San, to realize that there is still a place on the international circuit for this style of play.

## Stay square!

The way you position your body in relation to where you intend to hit the ball is a major factor which will enable you to glide easily between shots.

Ideally, you should be finishing most of your strokes with your shoulders and chest facing the point to which you are hitting the ball, known in the trade as 'square to the line of play'. To help you achieve this, your feet should also be pointing towards this same area. Gone are the days of Victor Barna when everything was 'side on', as it is in tennis. Because of the speed of today's game, you simply haven't got the time to indulge in such luxury.

Don't forget, though, that during a rally there are so many different variables at work, not least your opponent, his position, the ball, its speed, spin, and direction and your own state of readiness. It may not always be possible to get into exactly the right position, but nevertheless this should still be your aim.

*Make sure your shoulders finish facing square to the line of play.*

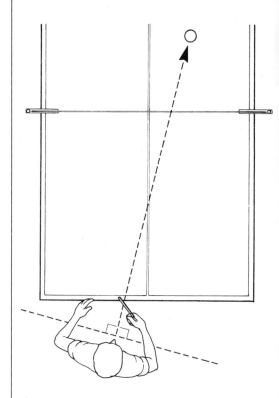

## Don't be just a ballwatcher!

What separates the great from the not-so-great in this game is the gift of anticipation. Those who have it are the game's clairvoyants, and seemingly can guess the future and known where the ball is going before you've even hit it. Sweden's Jan Ove Waldner and England's own Desmond Douglas are obvious examples. The rest of us are mere mortals who live in the present, missing chances and losing matches.

However, one of the reasons why some players remain mere mortals is that they only watch the ball. They could, if they applied themselves, elevate their status by developing their sense of anticipation.

Alison Gordon (England)

*The action for the backhand push.*

Watching the ball alone means you react far too late. Watching the opponent, on the other hand, and in particular his bat as well as the ball will provide vital clues about what is going to happen. This will give you that miniscule but nevertheless crucial bit of extra time which allows you to react earlier and help you seize the initiative.

# BASIC · STROKEPLAY

In the modern game, there is a core of four basic strokes which form the basis of every shot. They are:

1   the backhand push.
2   the forehand drive.
3   the backhand drive.
4   the forehand push.

From the drive strokes come all the topspin shots and their variations. From the push strokes comes the backspin or defensive, chopping style of play. You may well find that you have a greater aptitude for, say, the driving style than the pushing style, but don't think this excuses you from the need to master thoroughly all four. Only after this stage has been reached should your natural inclinations be allowed to give your game an identity.

Now, using just your elbow, move your bat forwards on a downward trajectory and stroke the back of the ball at the peak of its bounce. Your elbow should be at about an angle of ninety degrees as you make contact. Your follow-through should be smooth and short but not jerky or you will lose control over the length of shot. The backhand push, just like its forehand counterpart, is a soft delicate stroke used to control the ball at the beginning of a rally and to prevent the opponent from gaining any advantage. It should be played short and in such a way that the ball almost caresses the net as it glides across the table.

A good way of retaining maximum control over flight and direction is to keep your head close to the bounce of the ball as you perform the stroke. At the same time, use your free arm to point to the ball as an aid to co-ordination. Length is determined largely by making sure that your forearm and grip are suitably relaxed. If you find the ball is bouncing too high when it hits the other side of the table, check that you aren't hitting under it. This might be due to your bat angle which could be too open, thereby lifting the ball as you strike it. You will probably find that the optimum bat angle is around forty-five degrees off the vertical.

Avoid using your wrist at this early stage. The wrist becomes enormously important later when we come to look at spinning the ball. All the arm joints have a part to play in stroke production. In certain strokes, like the push, one joint, in this case the elbow, assumes the lead role, in other shots, like the forehand topspin, all three joints from the shoulder downwards must synchronize together to produce the finished article.

It's not too difficult to set up a series of table exercises which involve using only backhand push. The diagrams give you one or two examples to start with. Once you feel that you've mastered the basic principles of the technique, concentrate on achieving consistency in distance, height and direction.

## Backhand push

With all the pushing and chopping strokes, the bat needs to be held in what we term an open angle, in this case using the backhand side of the blade.

Start by facing the direction you want to play the ball – remember, square to the line of play – with your feet in line with your shoulders. Neither foot should be in front of the other. You should be close to the table but not leaning over it. The ball is played from directly in front of, or just to the left of your stomach, and under your chin. If the ball is moving wide, shift across to this position first before you start the shot.

# TABLE TENNIS

*Four exercises using only the backhand push.*

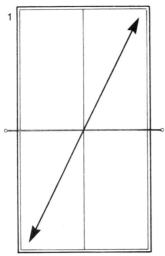

Using the diagonal, play the ball deep into each other's half of the table.

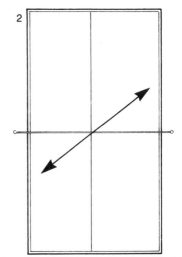

Now play it as short over the net as possible.

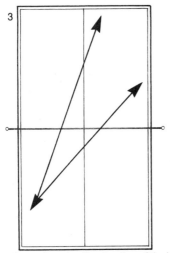

One player alternates the direction of the ball.

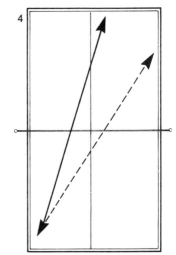

One player alters the direction at random – as shown by the dotted line.

## Forehand drive

We deliberately started with the backhand push because it's usually regarded as the easiest to learn of the four basic strokes. But there are no hard and fast rules which govern the order in which you gather your basic armoury of shots. There's a strong school of thought which takes the view that all novice players should learn to drive the ball before learning to push it. The rationale for this lies in the theory that, under pressure, you will keep your aggressive instincts, because driving and hitting the ball is the first thing you learnt all those years ago.

At certain times during a game, you will be presented with balls on which you must make a snap decision to push or to drive. The push will keep the ball safe but it's a negative sort of shot in this situation and it probably won't win you the point outright. The drive, on the other hand, represents a more positive approach; it's a bit more risky but only fractionally so and will undoubtedly give you a better chance of winning the rally. Only through practice will you find out what suits you best.

Let's turn our attention to the shot itself. The same principles of *finishing up* square to the line of play still apply, but with the forehand drive it usually helps if you *start* the stroke with a stance which is partly side-to-square. If you're a right-handed player, you should be leading a little with the left foot.

Make sure that your bat is being held with a slightly closed angle and your elbow is at about ninety degrees and at least 13cm (5in) away from your body. Think in terms of rolling a large hula-hoop along the road. Using your shoulder, move your bat forwards and upwards at the same time, hitting through the back of the ball at the peak of its bounce. Your bat should finish its follow-through roughly in line with your nose. To enable you to do this, your upper body should be rotating slightly from a side-to-square position to finish the stroke square. As a reminder, it sometimes helps if you gently grasp your playing wrist with your free arm as you're performing the stroke. This will have the effect of automatically pulling and rotating your upper body through to the finishing position.

At the same time, and as if you haven't got enough to think about already, your weight should be transferring from the back foot through to the leading, front foot. Its important to establish this principle of weight transference early on because it plays such an integral part at a later stage when you want to put power and speed into your game and be able to hit the ball harder.

When you first practise the forehand drive, use the forehand diagonal of the table to start with. The diagonals are the longest sections of the table and give you a greater margin of error to allow you to get the distance right. Remember, you should be hitting at the peak of the bounce with the ball clearly travelling in a downwards path to the other side of the net.

If you find that you're overhitting the end of the table, it could be because you are leaning back without realizing it. If this is so, it means that your bat angle will be wrong, resulting in your hitting under instead of over the ball.

What happens if the ball is wide? Answer: 'I stick my bat out and try to reach it.' Wrong! You don't reach in this game, not unless you are in dire trouble. Instead, you reposition yourself by moving your feet. This shouldn't be a problem because by this stage you'll have got yourself into the habit of keeping to

a good stance which allows you to spring around quite effortlessly.

## Backhand drive

At one time, it was possible for players to reach quite a high level in the game – a world ranking, even – largely on the strength of a powerful forehand drive and topspin. Their backhand only needed to be a containing stroke, and when an opening occurred on the backhand wing they would run around and put the ball away with their

*The action for the forehand drive. The stance is slightly side to square.*

forehand. Then, in the mid-Seventies, along came a new breed of players led predominantly by the Hungarians and the Swedes, who were strong on both wings and who could apply virtually the same amount of power and spin with their backhand as with their forehands. The forehand-only experts quickly disappeared from view, outmanoeuvred and outplayed by their more versatile successors. If you wish to achieve any degree of success, it is important that you also become strong on both wings.

Your approach to the stroke should be the same as for the backhand push – square and facing the area of the table in which you wish the ball to land. Make sure you don't lead with your right foot (assuming you're a right-hander) as this will make it difficult for you to shift across to your forehand wing. Unlike the push, though, this shot is played over the ball so a slightly closed bat angle is required.

With your elbow at an angle of about ninety degrees move the bat forwards and upwards by using your elbow joint, starting from a point which is just to the left of your

stomach. As you make contact – again, at the top of the bounce – try and let your wrist turn over the ball. The important point to bear in mind, is that the power for the backhand drive comes from the elbow; the wrist serves only as a finishing touch to guide the ball onto the right flightpath, which will be a downward trajectory. You might find it helpful to think of the stroke as trying to punch the ball with your knuckles but using only your forearm to do it.

For maximum control, keep your head over the ball and avoid reaching and therefore playing the shot outside of the line

of your body. If you find you're overhitting, check your bat angle, it may need closing a little more. Equally, if you're hitting into the net too often, open the bat until you find just the right position. Of course, you will also need to make fine adjustments to your bat angle depending on the speed of the ball.

*The action for the backhand drive.*

# TABLE TENNIS

*Four exercises using combinations of the forehand and backhand drive. FD = forehand drive, BD = backhand drive.*

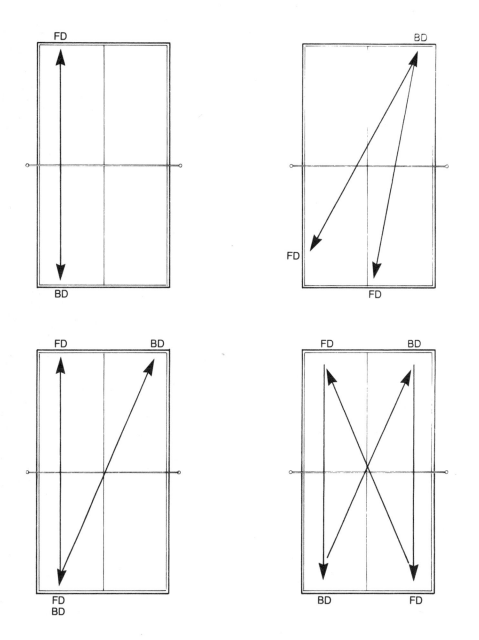

Andrei Mazunov (USSR)

*The action for the forehand push. If the ball is short don't be afraid to put your leading leg forward, under the table if necessary, to bring your upper body near to the bounce of the ball.*

# TECHNIQUE

## Building practice routines

You now have three strokes in your repertoire. Congratulations! In our experience this is more than many league players manage to develop in a lifetime – which is probably why they're still just struggling league players and nothing more. Let's take some time out to consider how you're going to develop and improve your game.

There are several practice routines you can use which involve just one stroke or combinations of two or more. It's important that you start piecing shots together as soon as possible because, after all, this is what a game situation is all about – a series of differing shots played in succession with the combined strategic aim of winning the rally. The diagrams on page 36 give you some suggestions, and as you become more proficient we have every confidence that you will soon be supplementing them with ideas of your own.

There are two ways of improving in any racket sport: one is by competition, in matches and tournaments, and the other is by practice. Although the latter may sometimes lack the glory and excitement of the former, you will soon discover that it's essential to fulfilling your true potential.

## Forehand push

It's fair to say that so far we have talked about the pushing strokes in terms of them being safety strokes – shots that give nothing away but at the same time gain very little. Don't be misled into thinking that they are somehow unimportant. There are certain balls where the only option available to you is to push, and if you can't keep it tight the result will inevitably be that you find yourself picking the ball up off the floor because it's just been smashed past you.

In many respects, the forehand push is probably the most awkward of the basic strokes to master but for the reasons we

have just outlined you would be well advised to persevere and conquer it.

Assume the same sort of stance as you would for the forehand drive, slightly sideways-on with your left foot leading your right (assuming you're right-handed). Because it's a pushing stroke you will need an open bat – not too open, just slightly off the vertical. Make sure that there's ample space between your elbow joint – which should be at about ninety degrees – and your upper body. A common mistake made by many players is that they tend to cramp the shot because their body gets in the way of their elbow movement. Now, with your head near to the bounce of the ball, move your bat forwards from the elbow and slightly downwards at the same time. You should be making contact at, you've guessed it, the peak of the bounce. To help you co-ordinate the stroke, you can use your free arm to point at the ball just as you might use a gunsight. Your follow-through should be short and the stroke should finish almost as soon as you've hit the ball.

Try to resist the temptation to scoop the ball. You can avoid this by making a point of letting the bottom edge of your bat scrape lightly against the table surface. If the ball is short, stick your right foot under the table to bring your upper body and bat arm closer to its bounce. In this way, you will be keeping maximum control over the whole process.

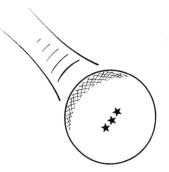

# MOVEMENT · AND · FOOTWORK

One of the most important aspects of play, helping you join the various strokes together, is footwork. You may have the most beautiful technique in the game but if you can't get around the table without falling over your feet, it will all be academic.

To cover ground when close up to the table and to be able to react quickly, most players use what we term 'stepping footwork'. This is characterized by the fact that the feet do not cross over one another. It's a sideways skipping or even a shuffling

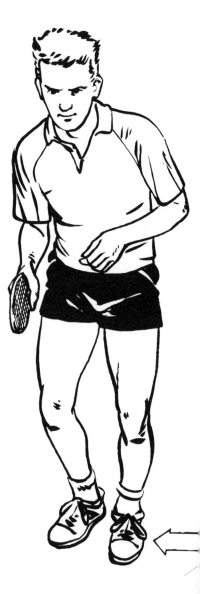

motion designed to leave you with the right stance – one where your feet will be as wide apart as your shoulders and your weight will be centred on the balls of your feet.

Crossing your feet when up to the table can be suicidal. Once crossed, you discover that your body has become immovably entrenched, sideways-on, making quick recovery to the opposite wing almost impossible. Sideways-stepping keeps you square and, as you will have discovered by now, for most shots this is how you need to be positioned.

Away from the table, when you're scrambling around with your back to the ropes, it's a different story. It is very difficult to move quickly without crossing the feet. However, because there is so much more distance between yourself and the table, there is also that little bit of extra time. You can afford, therefore, to run to the ball and this will obviously involve you in crossing your legs.

There are no definite and absolute rules about footwork and we are wary of coaches who preach along the lines of 'never' and 'always'. The reason being that we have been proved wrong so many times in the past. There are numerous examples of top-class players whose footwork at first sight appears to be a mess. But then, when you make a closer inspection, you discover that although their patterns may be unorthodox, they serve the player well without impeding mobility.

*Stepping footwork, when close to the table, will leave you well-balanced for each successive stroke.*

*If you cross your legs when close up to the table, it will be very difficult to recover if your opponent plays the next ball down your backhand.*

## How good is your footwork?

Let's take a typical situation which crops up during the course of most rallies. The ball is switched from your backhand, wide over to your forehand. Your response is to shuffle lightly across – using stepping footwork, of course – and while retaining a firm base, you reposition your right foot so that it trails your left slightly. Your body weight is balanced over to your right leg. You are now in the

classic position, ready to execute a devasting forehand drive. But wait a second! All this sounds too easy. This is what should be happening, but does it always turn out like this? How do we make sure that it does?

The answer lies in a technique known as 'irregular footwork exercises'. But before we can go on to look at this technique in detail, we need to look firstly at its counterpart, 'regular footwork exercises'.

## Regular footwork exercises

Put quite simply, a regular footwork exercise is a practise sequence in which the direction of the ball is varied but the receiving player knows where. For example, in a repeat sequence of two balls down the backhand, two to the centre and then wide over to the forehand. Because you know in advance when the changes in direction are going to occur, the footwork pattern you need to adopt to return each ball is comparatively easy to perform and establish. The predetermined nature of the exercise lets you groove the pattern into your subconscious to the extent that it becomes virtually automatic. Well, this is the theory anyway. We can test it, and whether you can now react to this situation automatically, by using an 'irregular footwork exercise'.

## Irregular footwork exercise

Irregular footwork exercises are a good way of recreating the rigours and uncertainty of matchplay. As you know, when you become involved in a game situation, the opponent will persist in that nasty habit of playing the ball to all parts of the table. And what's more, he doesn't even have the common decency to tell you where he's going to play each shot. An irregular footwork exercise should confirm whether your regular footwork patterns have invaded and established themselves in your subconscious.

A typical irregular footwork exercise would be one where the ball is played predominantly across the backhand diagonal, but your practice partner is allowed to switch one without warning down your forehand side. Try it. Did your feet move without you having to ask them or are you finding that you're still 'late for the bus'?

If it seems that you're failing to get there quick enough, check that you are not just 'ballwatching'. Start 'batwatching' as well, and give yourself a headstart. Remember,

anticipation might be the key that takes you out of the ordinary and into the extraordinary.

On the other hand, your apparently slow reactions may be attributable to your having rushed your development. You may have tried to master irregular practices without having first devoted enough time to more straightforward regular routines.

## Recovery

There is a further factor which can help you make maximum use of both your footwork and anticipation. It is the position at the table to which you recover immediately after you've played the shot. Of course, this will depend almost entirely on the area to which you have chosen to hit the ball and therefore the target area on your side of the table which becomes available to your opponent.

It sounds complicated, doesn't it, but really it's all a matter of common sense. Take a look at the diagram on page 44. You can see how the position and direction of the ball you have just played fixes the parameters of the target area now open to your opponent. Your aim should be to reduce the opponent's scope, wherever possible, and then recover to a position which is just to the left of or central to his available angle of play. From this position, you should then be

# TABLE TENNIS

*The angle you need to cover will depend on where you play the ball. This will vary continuously as the rally progresses.*

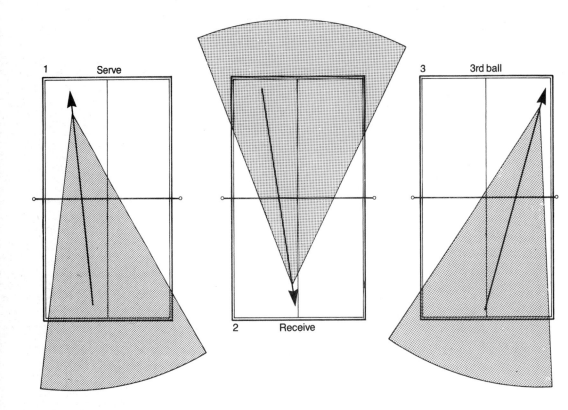

able to get to any ball he chooses to play. Too far over to the left of the available angle and you will be leaving yourself exposed on the forehand side (assuming you're a right-hander). Too far over to the right and you could be stretched on your backhand.

For some players, an appreciation of this principle may already exist because they are gifted, instinctive tacticians. If you don't fall into this category, it means that you have one more good habit to pick up on the tricky road to success.

Desmond Douglas (England)

# SERVICE · AND · RECEIVE

Table tennis is a sport littered with unfulfilled players who could quite easily put five points on their game if they devoted more time and attention to their service technique. In tennis, it is speed and power that gives the opponent his greatest difficulties in returning the serve. In table tennis it is the more gentle but no less threatening qualities of spin, length and disguise which blend together to apply the pressure.

But you will only become a master of the art of service – because that is what it has become, almost an art form – if you are prepared to practise and work hard at it. Look upon service practise as an investment that pays handsome dividends well in excess of the normal market rate. All those matches that you've been losing 21-18 or 21-19 could be turned the other way. Before you read on and learn how to acquire a good service technique, it may be worthwhile first

checking that you aren't in breach of any of the rules in this particular area. In the chapter 'The Game – A Guide' you will find a short section which covers the various service laws and this should help to refresh your memory.

## How to achieve a good service

In today's game, the type of service favoured by most top players is the 'two-bounce serve'. Essentially a short service, it takes its name from the fact that if the ball were allowed to continue its course, it would bounce twice on the receiver's side before falling away off the table. Ideally, the second bounce should occur on or about the receiver's baseline.

There are several reasons why this sort of serve has become so tactically advantageous:

*By making the ball bounce midway on your own side of the table, you should achieve a service of ideal length.*

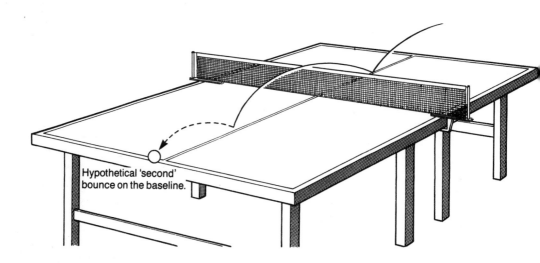

Hypothetical 'second' bounce on the baseline.

1   It is difficult for the opponent to push it back short and therefore keep the ball tight.
2   If the opponent does happen to push it long or even flick the ball, the target angle available is comparatively small. This leaves you as the server with a little extra time to anticipate the direction of the return.
3   The opponent is often caught in two minds. Is it long enough for an attacking topspin shot to be attempted or is it too short and should it be pushed?

And if they do decide to push it, you should have been able to impart enough spin on the ball in the first place to make it difficult to control.

Irrespective of whether you serve using your forehand or backhand, this type of service is achieved by following a few straightforward but relatively basic ground rules.

Firstly, make sure that the bounce on your own side of the table occurs midway between the baseline and the net. This means that the bounce on the opponent's side is also going to occur at the same midway point. This is the critical point which ensures that the hypothetical second bounce will then occur around the opponent's baseline.

Secondly, to control the height of the ball's bounce, you should be striking the ball at a point during its descent which is roughly the same height as the net, around 15cm (6in) or so. Common sense tells you that to hit the ball at a higher point will only result in an unwanted 'bouncy' serve which inevitably invites the attention of the opponent's smash.

Thirdly, and this is where the real skill comes in, you need to keep your wrist loose to allow the bat to brush quickly across the ball to make it spin. We shall be looking at the whole question of spin very shortly, but it is a factor which takes on vital significance in the area of service and receive. Not only is

it important that you are able to spin the ball, but your opponent must remain unaware throughout of the type of spin you have imparted and the ball's direction. In other words, you must acquire the skill of deception.

Lastly, as with any stroke, you need to recover – and this should be part of the service action – to the appropriate part of the table. Remember, we looked at recovery positions earlier as part of our examination of movement and footwork. If you choose to serve to, say, the opponent's forehand wing, the target area that opens up to him is your own forehand part of the table and vice-versa with the backhand.

## The serving action

Let's return for a while to the service action itself. We mentioned how important it is to keep your wrist relaxed and fluid. If you want to spin the ball, your bat has to be travelling fast, but you must convert this speed away from hitting into the ball, because this will probably mean that it will miss the table altogether. On the other hand your aim is to slice or drag the bat face pendulum fashion across the ball's surface. With this technique, which requires a dexterity, touch and feel that it can take years to fully develop, the bulk of the energy exerted becomes transformed into spin with only very little being needed to propel the ball forwards.

One of the most popular service techniques favoured by many top players is the **high toss serve**. The most spectacular exponents are undoubtedly the Asian players who seem to regard the height of the roof as the only restriction on how high the

ball is thrown. Twenty feet is by no means unusual and it is remarkable how well they control the fast accelerating descent of the ball and convert its speed into spin. From the opponent's point of view, this serve can be distracting and psychologically threatening. It looks fearsome and with skill it is possible to conceal the contact point of bat on ball with the free hand thereby disguising the type of spin which is being imparted.

We don't recommend that you necessarily spend the next six months trying to get to grips with this difficult service. You would be better advised on developing touch and feel on the ball with more modest services, with a consistent throw-up which is no more than a couple of feet in height at maximum. Try and get into the habit of relaxing the wrist and elbow joint and synchronizing them together. An open bat angle with the bat brushing across the ball will help you to maintain control over the pace of the service.

On the backhand side, keeping the head over the point of contact will help you attain the control necessary. On the forehand side, check that your throw-up is not resulting in the ball landing too far away from the body so that you end up having to reach. Another good tip is to relax your grip and let the base of bat handle fall from the heel of your hand so that the bat is being controlled almost entirely by your thumb and forefinger. This will aid the pendulum-like swinging action that you need to develop.

Once you are able to generate an appreciable amount of spin, start to experiment with varying the point of contact of the ball upon the bat. Using the outer sections of the blade can have the effect of increasing the amount of spin because these are the fastest moving parts of the bat. The centre of the bat will produce slightly less spin. This is worth knowing if you want to disguise your service and deceive the opponent into thinking that the ball is spinning viciously. If you happen to be skilful enough to become a master of disguise, it will quickly become apparent that no spin at all is often as useful as spin itself.

*The serving action for the forehand sidespin serve. Controlling the bat with just your thumb and index finger will enable you to brush the ball quickly as contact occurs.*

The serving action for the
backhand sidespin serve.

Jorgen Persson (Sweden)

*The action for the long backhand serve.*

## The long service

So far we have concentrated our attention on achieving the two-bounce serve but there is undoubtedly a place in today's game for a low fast service – the long service.

This clearly comes into its own when it is sprung on the receiver as a surprise. It's obviously important, therefore, that your body actions don't signal that a long serve is on its way. Your opponent should be kept guessing and it should only be at the moment immediately prior to contact that you adjust your serving action.

The main technical differences between the long and short services are as follows:

1   The ball should be struck about 10cm (4in) or so above table height.

2   The bounce on your side of the table needs to be fairly near to the baseline; this will ensure that it bounces deep in the opponent's half of the table.

3   Your bat needs to move just as fast as it does in the two-bounce serve, except that the energy and speed you exert is directed through the ball rather than across it.

The best time to slip in a long serve is when you detect from the corner of your eye that the opponent is slightly out of position. A sudden change in pace and direction might succeed in generating a loose return which you can then capitalize on.

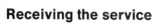

## Receiving the service

A philosophy of just returning the service and hoping the opponent will make a mistake is a certain way to lose games. In many ways it might be a reflection of your general attitude of mind which should be positive and *not* negative. When you're receiving the serve, the stroke you play must be a positive one, which has a definite purpose in mind. At the very least, your aim is to cancel out the advantage which naturally lies with the server and restore the balance. Some people believe that the term 'positive' means that the ball has to be smashed out of sight, but this is entirely unnecessary.

Here's a checklist of things to remember when you are returning the serve.

*Stance*   If your weight is on your heels what chance have you of moving quickly to the ball? Adopt a well-poised stance, facing the server with your bat pointing at the ball as it rests in the server's hand. As a general rule, position yourself in such a way that you can cover two-thirds of the table with your forehand and the rest with your backhand. Remember, though, that you might need to alter your position according to where the serve is coming from.

*Watch the server's bat*   If he throws the ball twenty feet into the air, ignore it. Keep your eyes firmly focused on his bat throughout and try to detect the direction and type of spin on the ball.

*The flick return is played over the table using the elbow and wrist.*

**Footwork** Assuming the serve is short, move your nearest foot to the ball, keep your playing arm slightly bent and your head near to the ball for maximum control. There is nothing wrong with moving the furthest foot first. It certainly has the advantage of bringing the shoulders round but it can leave you a little exposed on your backhand. Moving the nearer foot is a shorter movement, is comparatively easy to execute and for most players often feels the most natural method.

## Positive returns

What about the type of shot to use? Obviously, this will be a matter for your own intuition and judgment. It will also depend on the length of the serve but remember what we said about the need to be positive. Here are three positive returns to a short service which seem to be favoured by most leading players today:

**Short push** Using your wrist, take the ball at the peak of the bounce when it's at the same height as the net. Your bat should be slightly open and held comparatively loose to retain touch and control. Use the centre of the bat as the contact point and aim for within 30cm (12in) or so of the net.

**Fast attacking push** Again, take the ball at the top of the bounce but use your elbow together with your wrist to push it deep and fast. Your contact point should be the edge of the bat and you should aim into the receiver's playing shoulder or, if he's off-guard, play it wide.

**Flick** With a closed bat face, hit over the back or top of the ball using your wrist, supplemented with a little elbow action as well. The contact point should be the edge of the bat.

Your wrist plays a critical role in all three of these returns. With the last two, it's especially important that you develop a technique which allows the bat to move quickly through the ball to counteract the effect of the server's spin.

# *ADVANCED · TECHNIQUES*

To hit the ball hard or to spin it, you have to be able to generate power and speed of movement. You then need to be able to transmit this directly into the ball. If your basic technique is correct, this should be a comparatively straightforward process. If, on the other hand, you find that you're getting into difficulty, it may be that the foundations are not as strong as you thought. Running before you can walk is fraught with danger. Don't be afraid to 'return to go' and spend a little more time correcting a basic fault before you move on to the next stage.

## Producing power

Table tennis is a 'whole body skill'. So far, we have concentrated on how the joints of the upper body become synchronized to produce the right striking action. When it comes to producing power – for either spin or speed – you need to be able to incorporate the joints and stronger muscle groups in your legs and lower abdomen as well. Then, you must be able to transfer your body weight into the ball. Probably the only way to illustrate this principle effectively is to look at two of the more widely used power shots that feature in today's game.

## Fast forehand drive

This stroke is produced by accentuating many of the key features of the forehand drive. Start by making sure that your knees are bent a little more than they would be in the basic version. Your body weight should be supported predominantly by your back leg (which will be your right if you happen to be a right-hander).

Your upper body needs to turn to start the stroke from a more pronounced sideways-on position using your waist as a pivot. Lengthen your bat arm by increasing the angle at the elbow to around 120 degrees.

Start the stroke by pushing your weight forward from your right leg, through to your left. At the same time, your waist should be rotating to a position square to the line of play. This, in turn, will automatically start the process of drawing your bat arm forwards. Now, move your playing shoulder as well to increase the bat's speed. Finally, start to close your elbow and last of all your wrist. As with most attacking strokes, the timing point is the peak of the bounce. Make sure that your bat angle is such that you are hitting through the ball and not stroking or brushing it too much.

If all these joints have 'unlocked' themselves in the correct order your bat should now be moving like greased lightening! If it isn't, it could be that too much of your swing is taking the form of an elaborate follow-through. At least seventy per cent of the swing needs to occur before you get to the point of striking the ball and, most important of all, your bat needs to be accelerating at this point. There's nothing wrong with a follow-through – it's an integral part of any stroke – but keep it economical.

## Forehand kill

This stroke shares many of the characteristics of the fast forehand drive. The major difference is explained by the word 'kill', implying that the rally should be dead once you have completed this dynamic shot.

In technical terms, the transfer of weight from the back foot through to the front needs to be particularly emphatic if you are to hit the ball hard enough to produce the desired effect.

It is invariably used against a loose ball from the opponent – one which has little speed or spin and tends to bounce about mid-table. Make sure that you start the stroke with your bat held at the same height as the ball or, if the ball is bouncing too high, at shoulder height at the very least. This is because your bat needs to be moving on a downward plane to prevent you from overhitting the other side of the table. To call the forehand kill a 'stroke' is a misnomer; there should be no 'stroking' about it. All the energy and hatred you can muster must be transmitted straight through the ball.

## SPIN

An intuitive understanding of the effects of spin and how to handle it are essential to any devotee of modern table tennis. Being able to impart fantastic amounts of spin upon the ball is without doubt a very useful weapon. However, it is just as important to understand the effects of spin and have the skill to read it, neutralize it and thereby deaden its impact. A failure to develop these latter skills is a characteristic of many aspiring players – they might be able to dish it out but can they take it?

A table-tennis ball can be made to spin on its central axis by brushing the surface of the bat across it. For a split second the ball is gripped by the rubber and then rotated. This microsecond when this gripping effect occurs is often referred to as the 'dwell factor' or in some quarters 'the coefficient of friction'. Generally speaking, the stickier the rubber, the greater the dwell factor and in

*The action for the fast forehand drive. Make sure your bat angle is adjusted so that you hit through the ball.*

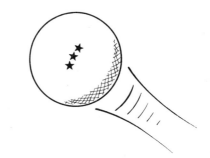

turn the greater the spin that can be produced.

A ball can be spun in any direction and this will be governed entirely by the direction in which the bat travels. Two types of spin tend to predominate in today's game: topspin, favoured by players with an attacking style, and backspin, preferred by defensive players. Sidespin is usually a hybrid version of these two forms of spin.

**Topspin** has the effect of making the ball dip downwards in its flight and then bounce suddenly forwards when it connects with the table surface. In tactical terms, the aim is to force a return which either misses the table completely or a loose, high ball which can be killed.

**Backspin** or **chop** is quite the opposite. If imparted correctly, it makes the ball hang in the air and stand up when it bounces. The common error made by most players dealing with backspin is to mistime the ball and, as a consequence, play it into the net. We will look at how backspin strokes are produced a little later (see page 62). In the meantime, let's return to our theme of power and speed and in particular how they become important elements in the production of topspin.

## Forehand topspin

A forehand topspin is produced in almost exactly the same way as the fast forehand

drive. The source of power lies in the leg muscles which start the process of acceleration in the bat arm. However, the rotation of the waist, the use of the shoulder and the closing of the extended angle at the elbow are also part of the movement. It is just like moving up through the gears of a car:

1 First gear: the legs.
2 Second gear: the waist.
3 Third gear: the shoulder.
4 Fourth gear: the elbow.

However, unlike the forehand drive where you are largely hitting into and through the ball, the bat is instead brushed lightly against it. This means that your bat angle needs to be adjusted and the trajectory of your swing will be more upward than through – about forty-five degrees to the floor. The faster you can move the bat, the faster you can make the ball spin.

It all sounds so easy when you read about it in a book but it's a different story in practice. The initial tendency of most players when they start out is to make the mistake of hitting the ball too much and not brushing it instead. Don't worry, this brushing action will eventually come to you. A useful tip is to keep your wrist fluid and relaxed in order to heighten your feel for the ball. At the crucial point of contact let the energy you have generated pass through your wrist, into the bat and onto the ball.

*The action for the forehand kill. Make sure you start your swing with the bat held above the height of the ball.*

*Backspin and topspin.*

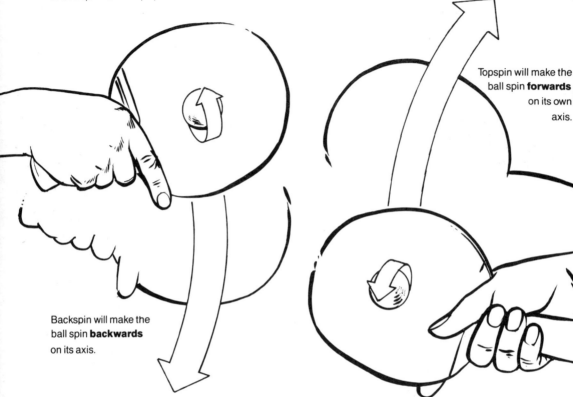

Topspin will make the ball spin **forwards** on its own axis.

Backspin will make the ball spin **backwards** on its axis.

## Fast and slow topspin

Many coaches talk in terms of fast and slow topspin. This can often become confusing because the descriptions 'fast' and 'slow' do not necessarily refer to the speed of the spin but usually to the speed of the ball. As we have already seen, power can be used for two purposes. One is for hitting the ball hard and thereby making it move rapidly through the air. Alternatively, it can be developed into making the ball spin. If we were to examine any given shot, we would probably find evidence of the two – speed and spin – combined together. Some of the energy you have produced will have gone into generating speed and propelling the ball forwards; the remainder will have gone into spin. The balance between the two will vary according to the manner in which you choose to strike the ball. The more you hit through the ball, the faster it will travel; the more you brush the ball, the greater it will spin.

The amount of spin you produce can be increased by brushing up the back part of the ball. With a more open bat angle this will have the effect of pronouncing the 'loop' in the ball's flight. In fact, it's quite common to hear of players using the nickname 'loop' to describe this shot. A well-executed loop will make the ball kick violently forward and upwards on its bounce. As with all topspin variations, your lower body and legs play a critical part with your bat held at a near-vertical angle. Instead of pushing your weight forwards, push it upwards. This will help to ensure that you brush the back of the ball. Use this loop drive against

*The action for the slow – or high – forehand topspin. Make sure your bat brushes the back of the ball.*

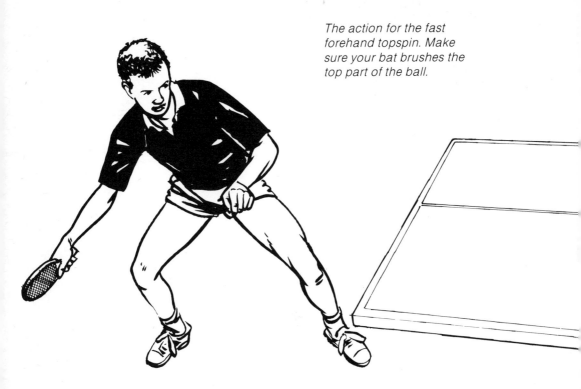

*The action for the fast forehand topspin. Make sure your bat brushes the top part of the ball.*

'choppers' – it can be a particularly effective method of combatting backspin, especially if you take the ball just after the peak of its bounce. In short, you will be capitalizing on the spin that's already on the ball and hopefully increasing it.

The fast forehand topspin is a different animal and almost invariably used in different circumstances. The bat angle needs to be very closed and the point of contact is on the top part of the ball so this means that your weight is thrown forward with your swing brushing the ball on an almost horizontal plane. This stroke is a powerful attacking way of returning a topspin ball. It has become popular amongst many of today's leading players whose high level of skill enables them to play it fairly early in the bounce. The opponent is placed under even greater pressure because he has less time in which to prepare an adequate response.

## Backhand topspin

Don't be misled into thinking that the backhand is somehow the poor relation as far as attacking spin shots go. Look at Andre Grubba of Poland or André Mazanov of Russia. Both are magnificent examples of players who can be equally as venomous on their backhands as their forehands. Anyway, if your opponent sees that you are incapable of opening the rally up on your backhand, that's precisely where he will concentrate his efforts. With the speed of today's game, the chances of compensating for a weak backhand by running round and using your forehand are remote.

It's not an easy stroke to master by any means. One of the main difficulties that most players encounter is generating sufficient speed to make the ball spin to any

*The action for the backhand topspin.*

significant degree. The reason for this is that the playing arm is shorter on the backhand than on the forehand simply because the bat is being held across the body. It follows, therefore, that you must look for ways of widening the arc of your swing. One way of doing this is to make sure that you start the stroke with your bat held just below knee height (and, of course, with your knees slightly bent). Keep your bat arm, and in particular your wrist, relaxed. To begin the

stroke, bring your bat upwards in line with your body weight which is jettisoned in the same direction.

Contact should occur just to the left of centre of your stomach by brushing the back of the ball at the peak of the bounce or just after. With this in mind, your bat angle should be slightly closed, just off the vertical. Although in most backhand strokes there should be hardly any rotation of the upper body, the backhand topspin, at very high

## Chopping, floating, blocking and lobbing

To an outsider these phrases must seem meaningless – to a table tennis player, they are part of the everyday vernacular. They complete the repertoire of strokes which form the technique of today's game. Not that any of them are recent innovations; 'chopping', or the backspin style of play, has been around for donkey's years and was particularly popular in the bygone era of Victor Barna, Richard Bergman and Johnny Leach. 'Floating' is a variation of the chop and is essentially a chopped ball in disguise, a ball that looks as though it's been played with backspin on it but in fact has no spin at all. Blocking is the technique of countering fast attacking and topspin shots by taking the ball, half-volley fashion, straight off the bounce. Lobbing is quite the opposite, an away-from-the-table form of defence that involves lofting the ball high into the air, deep into the opponent's half of the table with plenty of topspin. Let's examine each one in a little more detail.

*Chopping*   Look upon chop or backspin in much the same way as topspin except in reverse. Instead of brushing up or over the ball, you brush down the back or even under it. Whereas in the topspin game the power of the lower body is vital, it is of less relevance to the chopper. Positioning and anticipation, coupled with a judicious use of elbow and wrist, sum up the major requirements of this technique.

On both wings, start the stroke with your bat held at about shoulder height, with an open angle just off the vertical. Your elbow should be at around ninety degrees and your positioning should be a little away from the table. The timing point is just after the peak of the bounce and at about table height. On the backhand, stand fairly square to the line of play but turn so your playing shoulder is pointing to the ball. Using your elbow, slide the bat down the back of the

levels of competition, is the exception. If you're a right-hander, try turning slightly to the left and pointing to the ball with your playing shoulder. As you move through your swing, rotate your waist back to a position square to the line of play. This is another way of extending the arc of your swing and helping to increase the speed of the bat.

ball, brushing it outside your body but letting your shoulders rotate so that you finish square. You don't need much follow-through: as a guide, your elbow finishes the stroke not quite fully extended.

On the forehand wing, the same fundamental principles apply. Brush down the ball at about waist height, using a side-to-square stance but still rotating your shoulders so as to finish square. For good control, keep your head over the top of the ball as you strike it and try and transfer your weight through to your leading foot. This will help your recovery and leave you well poised for the next ball.

As with all strokes, there are no hard and fast rules governing the finer details of technique. Some 'choppers' play completely square because they find that a sideways-on approach leaves them vulnerable. By staying square throughout, it helps them move swiftly about the table, and switch between forehand and backhand with greater ease.

***Floating***   To be a successful 'chopper', you have to be able to vary the amount of spin you impart. The more you brush underneath the ball, the greater the spin. To do this you will need to keep your wrist loose, letting it snap clean just as contact is about to occur. Equally, you need to be able to force errors by floating the ball at opportune moments, particularly against players who you know like to loop it.

*The action for
the backhand chop.*

Floating is essentially the knack of discreetly hitting the back of the ball as opposed to brushing it. In all the other respects, the stroke must look exactly the same as a normal chop and lure your opponent into thinking that it's loaded with spin. The skill lies in altering your striking action at the very last second just as you connect with the ball. This is achieved by a disguised adjustment of your bat angle to bring it almost vertical and by tapping the ball lightly so that it returns spin-less. The follow-through completes the whole charade.

Chopping is often wrongly regarded as being defensive and negative. If all you end up doing is retrieving the ball with the same degree of spin every time and no variation you are hardly going to pose much of a threat. If, on the other hand, you can deceive and at the same time nip quickly into the table to kill any loose balls you will command far greater respect.

There is nothing negative or predictable about the great choppers Chen Xin Hua or Li Gun San, who are both quite capable of winning the world championship.

**Blocking**   Blocking is simply letting the ball rebound off your bat on the half-volley. Hardly any forward momentum on your part should be necessary. Instead, you work off the speed and pace generated by your opponent.

*The action for
the forehand chop.*

# TABLE TENNIS

*The contact point for
the backhand block.*

Your approach to either the forehand or backhand block is the same as that adopted for the forehand and backhand drives. The main difference is that you take the ball as soon as it bounces with your bat angle suitably closed to contain the speed and spin on the ball. Other fine adjustments of the wrist can be made to vary the direction of your returns.

Blocking is all about feel, so keep your grip relaxed, and watch the ball and your opponents carefully to assess whether there is much topspin on it. Try to make your returns as deep as possible into the other half to cut down the angles of play available.

Informed opinion on the merits or otherwise of blocking as a worthwhile technique is divided. However, if you anticipate well and take the ball quickly enough it can be a remarkably effective way of limiting the amount of time the opponent has to prepare for his next shot. Often, it can

be the only option available to you in dealing with a fast topspin ball and a good chance to manoeuvre him out of position.

**Lobbing**  It's quite remarkable to see how some of the game's great players, in particular Yugoslavia's Surbek and France's Secretin, have turned what amounts to a last-resort shot for most players into a deliberate match-winning tactic.

A high bouncing lob, played deep into the table with plenty of topspin, is undoubtedly a hard customer to deal with. A miserable-looking, dead ball that bounces halfway, on the other hand, is useless and will almost always get the treatment it deserves. It's important that you give the ball plenty of height because this will buy you the time to regain a better position. Play the shot in much the same way as a high topspin with the aim of getting it as near to the opponent's baseline as possible.

The action for the forehand
lob. Make sure you hit the
ball high into the air with
plenty of spin.

# INTO · BATTLE – TACTICAL · TIPS

As with most racket sports, there are those players who seem to have every shot in the book yet struggle against opponents who are technically inferior. Equally, there are those whose range of strokes is much more limited but who nevertheless get amazing results.

The rationale for this apparent contradiction probably keeps coaches, sports scientists and journalists and the like puzzling for years. No doubt the strange tricks played by the human mind could be a reason. Some players positively enjoy the tension and pressure that competition brings, whilst others fail to cope quite so well. Although a positive mental approach is absolutely vital, it's equally essential that you also develop a sound tactical awareness. Being technically proficient is one thing, but recognizing the right time to play the right stroke is a skill in itself.

## Warming up

Anxiety and an impatience to get on the table are invariably the reasons players overlook the pre-match warm up. This is a mistake because warming up is a key part of the tactical process.

Firstly, it stimulates the flow of blood around your system and enhances your flexibility. Table tennis is an explosive sport with most rallies lasting only a matter of seconds. There is no time for 'getting your eye in' once the match is underway so, physically at least, you need to be in a state of readiness as soon as the umpire says 'love-all'.

About five minutes before you are due on the table, seek out a quiet spot where you can privately run through a brief warm-up routine. Here's a typical example, but feel free to introduce your own modifications to suit your own physique and style of play. Keep your tracksuit top or a sweatshirt on throughout.

Start jogging gently on the spot for about a minute, keeping the rest of your limbs relaxed. Follow this with ten or so standing squats or perhaps thirty seconds of bouncing on the spot. These two exercises will make your heart pump a little faster because they involve the use of large muscle groups in the legs.

Now move on to a series of stretching and loosening exercises concentrating, in particular, on those muscle groups and joints which get the most use during a match. Here's a list of the type of exercises favoured by many of the England squad.

Working from the head downwards:

1   Neck rolling.
2   Straight arm circles from the shoulder, clockwise and anticlockwise.
3   Shoulder shrugs with arms by the side.
4   Upper body rotation from the waist with forearms held at shoulder height.
5   Hip circling with hands held at the waist (imagine you're using a hula-hoop).
6   Knee circling with the knees slightly bent and the legs held together. Rest your hands just above each knee to aid balance.
7   Roll the ankle joints by pivoting on your toe. One leg at a time.
8   Forearm circling from the elbow, clockwise and anti-clockwise.
9   Wrist rolling by clapping both hands together, 'prayer' fashion.

This brief warm-up routine – and shortly after the pre match knock up – will provide you with the opportunity to address your mind to the game in hand. Think about your opponent, his strengths and weaknesses. Can he handle spin? Is he quick about the table? How well does he react to changes in pace? If questions like these are running through your mind, then congratulations – you're thinking tactics.

Alan Cooke (England)

## Creating chances

Tactics is about using your weaponry to its greatest effect. An average point lasts between three and five seconds so it's important that you have a strategy which quickly exposes the opponent's weaknesses and either forces errors or gives you the upper hand to let you get in with a winner.

Let's start by looking at the area of service and receive because this is the earliest opportunity for you to fashion the rally to your own liking. Most players – at least at local league level – are weakest with a short serve to the forehand. This makes them stretch and in turn makes effective recovery against a fast third-ball attack hard to handle. Assuming your service has been sufficiently tight enough to produce a loose

Aim for this area here, between backhand and forehand wings.

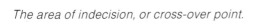

*The area of indecision, or cross-over point.*

return, topspin the ball either wide or into the opponent's 'area of indecision'. The area of indecision is that point where a player has to make a conscious choice about whether to play forehand or backhand. It will vary from player to player but the spot to aim for is around the playing shoulder. The top Korean and Olympic Champion Yoo Nam Kyu likes to cover around eighty per cent of the table with the forehand so, in this sort of situation, the cross-over point lies towards the backhand side. Players like Poland's Grubba or Mazunov of Russia are very strong on the backhand and will use it as often as possible. With this type of player, the cross-over point is more central, perhaps slightly towards the forehand side of the playing shoulder.

Think of your serves in terms of sets of five. If the weakness lies in the short serve to the forehand, for goodness sake don't play every one to this same spot. Within the first three serves, slip a fast one in, straight into the body, but make sure that it's disguised or its surprise effect will be lost. Although your aim will be to exploit the weak spot, wherever it may lie, use about three of the five services in this way.

With every serve you play, disguise, deception and unpredictability are pre-requisites. A serve with no spin can often be as effective in producing a loose return as one which is loaded with backspin, as long as the serving action looks exactly the same! Sweden's Jan Ove Waldner is a master at using this dummy 'float' serve at critical points in a match.

Counter-hitters can be vulnerable to long, heavily chopped serves because the subtle variation in pace and length can upset their rhythm. But again, don't allow them to get used to it – use it frequently but not repeatedly, as a way of reinforcing their uncertainty about how best to respond.

The type of return you play will depend both on the quality of the serve and your opponent's style of play. With short serves, the options are to push it short or to flick it. If you opt for the former against a good topspin player, make sure it's short enough to cancel out the advantage and stop them getting in with their loop. Against a counter-hitter or blocker, you may find that flicking the ball merely feeds the natural strengths of their game. Consider the occasional long push with plenty of backspin, deep into the body, as a useful alternative.

Where you return the ball is as important as what you do with it. As a general rule, avoid playing straight to the bat – play it deep or short and play it wide or into the playing shoulder. Mid-table balls straight to the bat are asking for trouble!

## Playing with your head

Most rallies go on beyond the second ball, that is, the serve is returned and a rally starts to open up. From then on, your tactics should be governed by your assessment of the opponent's strengths and weaknesses. So many players go on to the table clueless about how they intend to proceed. Playing to the weaknesses but avoiding strengths is a matter of simple common sense perhaps, but sound experience shows that it cannot be emphasized enough.

Before we go on to look at how to deal with various styles of play, here are a couple of instances where simple common sense is often the best tactic.

Take for example the typical situation of a player who has successfully forced his opponent back from the table. He is dominating the rally to such an extent that a bookmaker would probably say the player is in a ninety per cent win situation. Forceful smashes around the table or a carefully judged drop shot should secure the point without too much trouble. Instead, the player opts for the much more difficult and spectacular technique of driving the ball straight off the bounce, which is a fifty-fifty shot at the best of times. Let's assume that it goes on and the crowd go mad.

Logic tells you that with the odds so much in your favour, why on earth play such a risky shot? And what's more, the crowd's jubilant reaction to this undoubtedly spectacular stroke only serves to reinforce in the player's mind that it is the best ploy when faced with this situation in the future. The time to go for a difficult winner is when the odds are against you, for example when the opponent is in a seventy or eighty per cent win situation and when simple retrieval is likely to prove insufficient. This is the time to take a risk. If it comes off then so much the better, because it is likely to have the effect of psychologically disarming your opponent who will be shocked at your apparent ability to come back from the dead.

At local level, table tennis is characterized by players who are stronger on their forehand side and slightly weaker on their backhands. This common situation provides us with our second illustration to how an uncomplicated common-sense approach works best.

The most favoured tactic against a player with a weak backhand is to confine the play to this area of the table. However, this is a misconception. You will usually find that your opponent has compensated for his inadequacies and is adept at picking off balls played repeatedly to the backhand by shuffling round to use his stronger forehand.

To exploit a weak backhand, you first have to force the player into an exposed situation where a backhand return becomes an unavoidable shot. To achieve this look for a chance to flick or push the ball wide to the forehand first and then block or drive the return over to the backhand.

## Playing against different styles

Here's a brief synopsis of the strengths and weaknesses of differing styles of play. They have been broken down into three broad areas: topspinners/loopers,
counter-hitters/blockers,
defenders/choppers.

## Topspinner/looper

**Strengths**  Loopers are invariably adept at gaining maximum value from the third ball as a way of starting their attacking strategy. The continual use of spin makes it difficult to create an opening or take the initiative away from them. If they are clever enough to vary the level of speed and spin as well, they become even more awkward to handle. Chopping the ball without variation only serves to increase the amount of topspin they generate.

**Weaknesses**  The continued use of long strokes is physically demanding and slightly more time is needed to recover and be in position for the next ball. Blockers should therefore try to spread the ball around and avoid feeding the ball straight to the bat, particularly on return of service. Loopers can also be vulnerable to changes in pace and in particular to the floated ball. Both these techniques can have the effect of upsetting their timing. For choppers, it is vital to use variation and deception and not simple retrieval.

## Counter-hitter/blocker

**Strengths**  Great counter-hitters/blockers are characterized by their speed of reaction and highly tuned sense of anticipation. They control the ball well and thrive on the opponent's speed and topspin. Skilled exponents are usually capable of putting away a loosely played mid-table ball by taking it straight off the bounce.

**Weaknesses**  Blockers can be vulnerable to changes in pace and spin. Topspinners should switch between fast and slow topspin played deep into the other half of the table. Being predictable will only feed a blocker; instead, try and upset their appetite by changing the rhythm. For choppers, this is best achieved by interspersing severe backspin with a tempting float played into the body.

## Choppers/defenders

**Strengths**  Patience, tenacity and consistency coupled with a never-say-die attitude are the trademarks of a chopper and make this style of play one of the most frustrating to play against. Good choppers will vary the spin and try to deceive; they will also be prepared to spring quickly into the table and kill any loose, negative balls. Most choppers use a combination bat of reversed rubber on one side and pimples on the other which helps obtain a different effect on the ball.

**Weaknesses**  Choppers need to be worked hard during a match. Bring them into the table and drive them away from it, switch constantly between wings and topspin, fast and slow. Above all, watch both bat and ball closely. If the whole of the bat face is visible as it strikes the ball, watch out, it could be floated. Double-check by seeing if you can spot the manufacturer's mark on the ball. If it's visible, there's hardly any spin on it, so flat-hit it instead of topspinning.

# DOUBLES

The doubles game has been sadly neglected in recent years. This has been a costly error for many teams because in team or league play the outcome of a doubles contest can often decide a match.

There is a great tactical dimension to successful doubles, not only in terms of your choice of partner, where styles need to complement each other, but also in the order of play. Remember, in table tennis doubles, unlike its counterparts in other racket sports, the players must hit the ball alternately. Who you serve to in the first game – and, in effect, play every subsequent shot at – will not be the player you serve to in the second. This is because the Laws require you to change the pattern of play between each game. And if the contest goes to a third-game decider, the pattern must be changed again, when the score reaches 10, by the receiving pair changing places once more.

If you win the toss, bear this in mind when deciding whether to serve or not. It might be wiser to elect to receive and pass the right to serve to the opposing pair. Alternatively, you then choose which one of you receives, once the opposing pair have chosen which one of the two of them will serve.

If you happen to know that one of them is weak against topspin, and you happen to possess a fearsome loop, arrange it with your partner in such a way that you will be playing to the weaker player. You may feel it more appropriate to delay this arrangement until the second game, working on the principle of sneaking the first game and applying greater pressure in the second; and in the process romping away with a sudden 2-0 straight-games victory!

## Perfect your partnership

A good doubles partnership is like a good marriage and shares many of the qualities that are supposed to be the hallmarks of nuptial heaven.

The styles of the two players must **complement** each other, for example two attackers or two choppers. It's unusual for a defender and an attacker to be able to get it together and you will find that the divorce rate is high amongst these couples. The same applies to a half-volley blocker paired with an attacker. The usual drawback with this particular combination is that the attacker is less adept at absorbing speed and spin than the blocker, whose style of play by its very nature will generate fast returns which combine both these elements.

**Co-operation** is important. Doubles is about pooling your collective resources to maximum effect. Two good singles players

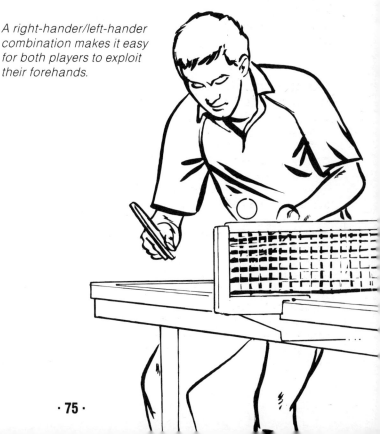

*A right-hander/left-hander combination makes it easy for both players to exploit their forehands.*

do not automatically make a dynamic duo; there is little room for selfishness; and acceptance of to the need to create openings and not always wanting to be the one who plays the winners are essential. Remember that both the type of stroke you play and its direction will have a bearing on the sort of ball your partner gets in return, and where it will have to be played from. Similarly, when you are awaiting your turn to strike the ball you must watch closely and carefully and try to anticipate the lines of play that are likely to occur.

**Consultation** is necessary. You can't go through a game without talking to one another; don't be afraid to exchange views and review pre-match strategies if they do not seem to be working out.

**Co-ordination** is required. The way you move around between strokes is vital in order to capitalize on the full range of strokes in your repertoire. This will be impossible if you are unable to keep out of

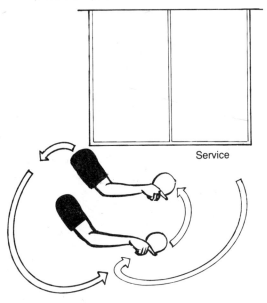

Service

*Two right-handers must circulate around each other and gravitate toward the left-hand part of the table to capitalize on the chances to use their forehands.*

one another's way. In this respect a pairing of left-hander and right-hander is the table tennis equivalent of Fred Astaire and Ginger Rogers. Such a combination should allow for both players to cover the table in a natural fluid way making maximum use of their forehands and cutting down the chances of being pushed wide into a position where a desperate backhand retrieve becomes the only option.

A partnership of two right-handed attacking players must learn to circulate. This involves moving out of each shot to the right, drifting away from the table and returning to a waiting position towards the left. This leaves you in the desired position of being able to cover at least sixty per cent of the table with your forehand. If you choose to serve with your forehand you can opt to move straight out to the left. If you prefer this approach, it is essential that you move quickly and immediately so you do not impede your partner's view of the return. This also applies if you choose to receive service with your forehand.

The obvious alternative to this strategy is for the server, or receiver, to move immediately out to the right. The chances of blocking your partner's view are reduced, but it means that your have to be especially nippy on your feet in the meantime if you are going to take up a ready position toward the left of the table.

As far as serving goes, your overall aim is still to be as unpredictable as possible but try and avoid a long service. As you should know by now, the main advantage to be gained from this type of service is that of surprise. In doubles, your line of service is predetermined by the Laws in that you must serve diagonally from the right into the opposition's own right-hand half of the table. Because of this, the opportunity for surprise is virtually minimal. Not only that, a long serve, especially against an attacker, is likely to bring a fast spinning return which will place your partner under unnecessary pressure at an early stage in the rally.

# USEFUL
# ADDRESSES

**English Table Tennis Association**
Queensbury House
Havelock Road
Hastings
East Sussex TN34 1HF
Tel: Hastings 722525

**Irish Table Tennis Association**
46 Lorcan Villas
Santry
Dublin 9
Tel: Dublin 791386

**Irish Table Tennis Association
(Ulster Branch)**
c/o Sports Council for N. Ireland
House of Sport
Upper Malone Road
Belfast BT9 5LA
Tel: Belfast 661222 ext 243

**Scottish Table Tennis Association**
18 Anslee Place
Edinburgh EH3 6AU
Tel: Edinburgh 225 - 3020

**Welsh Table Tennis Association**
198 Cyncoed Road
Cardiff CF2 6BQ
Tel: Cardiff 757241

**European Table Tennis Union**
43 Knowsley Road
Bolton
England BL1 6JH
Tel: Bolton 42223

**International Table Tennis Federation**
53 London Road
St Leonards-on-Sea
East Sussex TN37 6AY
Tel: Hastings 721414

# RULES CLINIC
# INDEX

Jan Ove Waldner (Sweden)

# INDEX